Novels for Students, Volume 26

Project Editor: Ira Mark Milne

Editorial: Jennifer Greve

Rights Acquisition and Management: Margaret Chamberlain-Gaston, Leitha Etheridge-Sims, Kelly Quin, Tracie Richardson Manufacturing: Drew Kalasky

Imaging: and Multimedia Lezlie Light Product Design: Pamela A. E. Galbreath, Jennifer Wahi Vendor Administration: Civie Green

Product Manager: Meggin Condino

© 2008 Gale, a part of Cengage Learning Inc.

Cengage and Burst Logo are trademarks and Gale is a registered trademark used herein under license.

For more information, contact
Gale
27500 Drake Rd.
Farmington Hills, MI 48331-3535

Or you can visit our Internet site at http://www.gale.com

ALL RIGHTS RESERVED. No part of this work covered by the copyright hereon may be reproduced or used in any form or by any means—graphic, electronic, or mechanical, including photocopying, recording, taping, Web distribution, or information storage retrieval systems—without the written permission of the publisher.

For permission to use material from this text or product, submit a request online at www.thomsonrights.com. Any additional questions about permission can be submitted by email to thomsonrights@thomson.com.

Permissions Department
Gale
27500 Drake Rd.
Farmington Hills, MI 48331-3535
Permissions Hotline:
800-730-2214
Fax: 800-730-2215

Since this page cannot legibly accommodate all copyright notices, the acknowledgments constitute an extension of the copyright notice.

While every effort has been made to ensure the reliability of the information presented in this publication, Gale does not guarantee the accuracy of the data contained herein. Gale accepts no payment for listing; and inclusion in the publication of any organization, agency, institution, publication, service, or individual does not imply endorsement of the editors or publisher. Errors brought to the attention of the publisher and verified to the satisfaction of the publisher will be corrected in future editions.

ISBN-13: 978-0-7876-8683-3
ISBN-10: 0-7876-8683-2
eISBN-13: 978-1-4144-2933-5
eISBN-10: 1-4144-2933-9
ISSN 1094-3552

Printed in the United States of America
10 9 8 7 6 5 4 3 2 1

Doctor Zhivago

Boris Pasternak

1957

Introduction

Boris Pasternak's *Doctor Zhivago* was first published in 1957, not in Pasternak's homeland, the Soviet Union, but rather in Italy. Pasternak's manuscript for this novel had to be written in secrecy and then smuggled out of the Soviet Union because of government censorship of Pasternak's work. Pasternak, as the author espouses through his protagonist, Yuri Zhivago, in this his only novel, believed that art should not be enslaved by politics and thus criticized his oppressive government through his writing.

Doctor Zhivago is an epic work that provides several fictionalized eye-witness accounts of the upheaval in Russia as the tsar is deposed, communism rises from the revolution, and a Marist government attempts to take control. *Doctor Zhivago* is also a love story of a man torn between two women—his wife, Tonia, and the beautiful Lara with whom Yuri has an affair. This novel explores the idealism of its protagonist, which is contrasted with the brutal reality of war and its effects on ordinary citizens. This work of fiction is also a philosophical treatise on life, religion, and art as expressed by its protagonist. Finally, Pasternak, who was also a poet, wrote *Doctor Zhivago* in a particularly lyrical style. Much of the text reads like poetry.

Critics, over the years, have had trouble classifying the work since in certain ways it does not conform to the conventions regarding novels. Pasternak often introduces characters who quickly disappear. The author often jumps forward in the story before solving present mysteries and sometimes focuses more on language and philosophical thought than on developing the plot line.

Despite some of these characteristics, *Doctor Zhivago* draws readers inside the lives and thoughts of its characters, their hopes and frustrations, their disappointments and their passions as they live through the Bolshevik Revolution and the creation of the Soviet Union, as a new world order under communism is attempted. One of the messages that

Doctor Zhivago delivers is that some dreams are never realized.

Pasternak was awarded the Nobel Prize for this novel. First published in Italian, the work was translated into many different languages and its story served as the basis for film and television dramas. After Pasternak died in 1960, the novel was finally accepted into the Russian literary canon.

Author Biography

Boris Pasternak was born in 1890 in Moscow to professional artists. His father was a painter who illustrated the works of famed Russian novelist Leo Tolstoy, and his mother was a concert pianist. Pasternak grew up surrounded by outstanding artists; for example, the poet Rainer Maria Rilke was a frequent visitor in his home.

Pasternak was well educated in the liberal arts. He studied art, music, and philosophy, but his first love was poetry. His first collection of poetry was published in 1914 but went unnoticed. Almost a decade later, however, Pasternak gained the public's attention with his poetry collections *Sestra moya zhizn* (My Sister Life, 1922), and *Temy i variatsii* (Themes and Variations, 1923). Although his novel received more attention in the United States, Pasternak is mostly remembered in Russia for his poetry.

Pasternak was fascinated by the Russian Revolution of 1905, and unlike many of his contemporaries, he did not emigrate to another country to escape the violence. He had studied philosophy in Germany and was inspired by the writings of Karl Marx (1818-1883), made famous by his book *Communist Manifesto* (1848), and the political activist and writer Maxim Gorky (1868-1936). Details of the war and some of his own experiences during the revolution found their way into Pasternak's poetry, as well as his only finished work of fiction, *Doctor Zhivago*. However, as the revolution continued and the brutality of the new government became obvious to him, he slowly retreated from politics. In addition, the Leninist attitudes present in the Russian government ran contrary to Pasternak's. Leninists believed that art should glorify and bolster the government, whereas Pasternak believed that art should seek the higher truths in order to benefit society. After Lenin's death in 1924, when Stalin came to rule, the clamp down on artists became more severe. The communist leaders demanded adherence to their rules and banned writers who did not agree that all art was to be used to promote communist ideals. Pasternak wrote an autobiography in 1931 called *Okhrannaya gramota* (Safe Conduct).

Pressure from government censorship intensified, so that when Pasternak decided to write his anti-Marxist novel, he had to do so in secrecy. When it was finished, he had it smuggled out of the country to Italy, where it was first published in 1957. The following year, Pasternak was awarded the Nobel Prize for Literature, but he was forced to refuse the award by the Russian government. He was thrown out of the official Union of Soviet Writers that same year and was threatened with exile. Instead, Pasternak pleaded with officials to allow him to remain in his beloved homeland. He lived out his remaining years in a colony of artists outside Moscow.

Pasternak was married twice. In 1922, he

married Evgeniia Vladimirovna Lourie. They had one son. The marriage ended nine years later. In 1934, he married Zinaida Nikolaevna Neigauz, upon whom the character of Lara in Pasternak's novel is based.

Pasternak died on May 30, 1960, of lung cancer. In 1988, the Union of Soviet Writers reinstated him, which opened the path for Pasternak's son to officially accept his father's Nobel Prize the following year.

Plot Summary

Chapter One: The Five-O'clock Express

Paternak's *Doctor Zhivago* begins with the funeral of the protagonist's mother. Yura Zhivago (who is called Yurii once he becomes an adult) is taken away by his maternal uncle, Nikolai Vedeniapin (or Uncle Kolia), whom Yura admires. Nikolai is a defrocked priest, cast out of the priesthood supposedly for his radical political views. He becomes, later in this book, a well known author, mostly of philosophy tinged with political theories.

Background information is given. Yura's father, a businessman, was very wealthy. Many buildings and streets in the town where Yura lived with his mother were named Zhivago, illustrating the influence that his father once had. Yura's father, however, was seldom at home. Yura discovers later that his father had a mistress and squandered the family's wealth. Yura's sickly mother often traveled in southern European countries in an attempt to cure her consumption. Yura, by the time of his mother's death, was used to living in the homes of many different people.

The chapter jumps ahead to 1903. Yura is still with his uncle. They visit another author whose work Uncle Nikolai has edited. Nikolai reminds Yura of his mother, "his mind moved with freedom and welcomed the unfamiliar." In this chapter, Pasternak initiates one of the main themes of this novel: the importance of the individual. Uncle Nikolai explains his belief that only the individual can express truth. But political thought in Russia at the time so subscribes to the group that Nikolai fears that outcome will be mediocrity. Uncle Nikolai suspects that many people grab on to one idea and stick with it regardless of its value.

Media Adaptations

- David Lean directed Robert Bolt's screen version of *Doctor Zhivago* in 1965, which was a box office hit. Omar Sharif played Zhivago, and Julie Christie played Lara. The movie won five Oscars.
- In 2002, *Doctor Zhivago* was

- adapted to a television script for British television.
- In 2003, *Masterpiece Theatre* presented a television version of *Doctor Zhivago*. Scottish actor Hans Matheson played Zhivago, and Keira Knightley played Lara. This version is available on DVD.
- As of 2007, a Spanish audio tape, *El Doctor Zhivago* (2005), was available. It was narrated by Philip Madoc.
- The Nobel Prize committee maintains a Paternal web page at http://nobelprize.org/nobel_prizes/literat with links to other interesting sites.

Also introduced in this chapter is Misha Gordon, a boy about the same age as Yura who becomes Yura's lifelong friend. Misha is traveling with his father on a train. On this same train is Yura Zhivago's father, who eventually throws himself onto the tracks, committing suicide. Also on this train is a character that prevails in the novel, Victor Komarovsky, a lawyer. It is suspected that Komarovsky affected Yura's father's suicide, by fostering the older man's excessive drinking and leading him to financial ruin.

Chapter Two: A Girl from a

Different World

An indeterminate amount of time has passed. Larisa (Lara) Guishar and her family, the widowed Amalia Guishar (Lara's mother) and Rodia (Lara's younger brother), are introduced. Russia is involved in a war with Japan (which Russia will lose) and the somewhat unorganized and sporadic revolutions of its citizens. The Guishars have just arrived in Moscow. Amalia has some money left from her husband's estate, but the sum is fast dwindling. She has asked Victor Komarovsky (who was at one time her husband's lawyer) to help her invest the money. Amalia buys a sewing shop and lives in one of the poorest sections of the city in order to extend her funds. She also has an affair with Komarovsky.

Lara, sixteen years old and just coming into her womanhood, notices the way Komarovsky looks at her, and this makes her very uncomfortable. However, as Komarovsky continues to focus on her, Lara is torn between hating him and being flattered by his attention. Komarovsky takes her out to dinner one night and makes a sexual pass at her. She turns him down initially but later gives in. Komarovsky is fascinated by Lara for her beauty, her intelligence, and her wild nature. Komarovsky scares Lara, and she despises herself for giving in to him.

Later in the chapter, Kuprian Tiverzin is introduced. He will later become a revolutionary. At this point of the story, Tiverzin becomes involved in one of the first labor strikes as the revolution gains momentum. Tiverzin has been identified as one of the leaders of the strike, and his mother warns him to run away. Pasha Antipov, the son of one of the managers of the railroad, seeks Tiverzin's mother, asking her to give him shelter since his father has been imprisoned.

A mass demonstration is organized; throngs of people crowd the streets, intent on rallying and protesting in front of the tsar's winter quarters. Tiverzin's mother takes Pasha with her as she joins the marchers. Cossacks, the tsar's military guard, surround the demonstrators and shoot indiscriminately into the crowd. Tiverzin's mother is punched in the back but not seriously injured.

Yura's uncle Nikolai has been published and is now very much in demand, giving lectures and teaching courses. He has left Yura in the care of the Gromekos. Alexander Gromeko is a chemistry professor. His wife, Anna, is the daughter of Ivan Krueger, a rich industrialist. The Gromekos have a daughter, Antonina (Tonia). Misha Gordon has also been left with the Gromekos, so Yura, Tonia, and Misha all live together through their adolescent years. Nikolai comments on how the three teens share beliefs about sexuality, how they think it is vulgar. Nikolai believes the youths have gone too far in their condemnation of sex.

Lara meets Pasha and notices that the boy has a crush on her. She watches him play with friends as if they are soldiers.

Lara hears that the area of Moscow where she

and her mother live will soon be under attack. She and her mother pack their things and move to a cheap hotel outside the district. Lara is happy about the move because she hopes this will keep Komarovsky away from her. Her mother, however, is disheartened when her workers go on strike. Lara fears that her mother may attempt suicide if she learns that her daughter is having an affair with Komarovsky.

One night, a doctor who is visiting the Gromekos (where Yura is living) is called to the hotel. Amalia Guishar has indeed attempted suicide by swallowing iodine. No motive is mentioned. Since the doctor was at the Gromekos when he was called, Yura and Misha ask to go to the hotel with the doctor for the adventure of it. This is the first time that Yura sets eyes on Lara, and he is taken by her, although he does not speak to her. Yura also senses that there is some dark secret between Lara and Komarovsky, but this intuition only makes Lara more intriguing. Yura also realizes that his physical response to Lara is related to what he, Misha, and Tonia have been talking about, the vulgar or sexual side of human interactions. Misha tells Yura that Komarovsky acted as Yura's father's lawyer, the man who might have been responsible for Yura's father's suicide.

Chapter Three: The Sventitskys' Christmas Party

Yura is in college studying medicine. He tries

to improve the health of Mrs. Gromeko, who has become bedridden. During one of the last talks she has with the two young adults, Anna Gromeko tells Tonia and Yura to become engaged. They are made for one another, Tonia's mother tells them.

Lara has moved in with a friend's family, the Kologrivovas, in an attempt to get away from her mother and Komarovsky. She is working as a tutor for the Kologrivovas's youngest daughter. While there, Lara's brother shows up and asks Lara for money. The only source of help that Lara can think of is Komarovsky. She finds out that he is at a Christmas Party, and Lara goes there uninvited. She has a gun with her. She sees Komarovsky playing cards with some other men. Lara shoots at him but misses, the bullet grazes another man's hand. Komarovsky later goes to court with Lara and helps to clear the case. Yura and Tonia were at the Christmas party, too. Yura is once again startled by and attracted to Lara. When Yura and Tonia return home, they find that Tonia's mother has died.

Chapter Four: The Hour of the Inevitable

Lara and Pasha marry. Both have now graduated from college and decide to take jobs in a small town, Yuriatin, in the Ural Mountains in western Russia. Meanwhile, Yura has his medical degree. Referred to as Doctor Zhivago or Yurii, he is working at a hospital on the front lines of World War I, where Russian and Hungarian troops are fighting. Yurii is married to Tonia, and she is about to have their first baby, a son.

Lara and Pasha also have a child, a three-year-old daughter, Katenka. Pasha is uncomfortable in his married life and decides to join the army. After joining, Pasha realizes he has made a mistake but it is too late to turn back. Later, rumors spread that Pasha has been taken prisoner. Other rumors state that he is dead. Lara, in the meantime, has decided to go to the frontlines to look for Pasha, to discover the truth of his whereabouts. She ends up working as a nurse in the same hospital as Yurii. At this point in the story, the human cost of war is unveiled as wounded soldiers flood the base hospitals. When Yurii is hit with shrapnel, Lara takes care of his wounds.

Chapter Five: Farewell to the Old

Chapter five begins in the town of Meliuzeievo. Lieutenant Galiullin is working with Yurii and Lara. Galiullin was once a friend of Lara's husband, Pasha. He has told Lara that Pasha was taken prisoner, but Lara does not believe it.

In a letter to Tonia, Yurii has mentioned Lara. In Tonia's reply, she insinuates that Yurii has fallen for Lara. Yurii is embarrassed about leading Tonia to feel this way, and he decides to make sure that Lara does not believe the same thing. Yurii appears unaware of his own emotions.

Meanwhile, revolutions and counter-revolutions occur all over the country. Government officials become increasingly ruthless, determined to stop the insurgencies. Court martials and death penalties that had once been rescinded are now in practice again. There are thousands of deserters: Soldiers are tired of war. Dissention brews among the Bolsheviks and between the Red and the White armies.

Yurii is distracted by wanting to confront Lara and make sure that she has not interpreted any of their conversations as his having an interest in her. In the midst of a philosophical discussion with Lara, however, Yurii exposes his true feelings toward her, as if the words just come out through their own will. He is embarrassed. Lara tells him to stop talking. She is about to leave to go back to Yuriatin. Yurii plans to return to Moscow. They part without further discussion.

Chapter Six: The Moscow Encampment

Yurii is home at last in Moscow. He must reacquaint himself with his son. His wife and her father are living in an old family home. Food is scarce and so is fuel; sporadic fighting breaks out in the streets. Yurii is reunited with old friends, but he is disappointed by how dull everyone looks. They are afraid of new ideas. Misha Gordon is there, playing a role that seems artificial to Yurii. Even Yurii's uncle Nikolai appears detached from what is happening around him. Yurii feels like a stranger in Moscow, someone who cannot fit in.

Much of this chapter deals with the everyday experience of hunting for wood for the furnace and whatever food Yurii and Tonia can find. The struggles are ongoing. However, Yurii holds out hope that this is part of the process of creating a new world order. He still has dreams that the communist system will adjust, and life will become easier.

Yurii contracts typhus, a disease carried by the ticks and fleas on rats. While he is unconscious with fever, his half-brother, Evgraf, brings the family food and other supplies. Yurii does not even know Evgraf. However, Evgraf is well aware of Yurii, having heard of Yurii's good works. Evgraf admires him. When Yurii is healthy again, he realizes that his time in Moscow has come to an end. It is now about 1917, and he does not accommodate the restrictions and the group-think style of the new Soviet Union. Yurii is an individual, and his forward-thinking ideas come up against the prescribed communist values. He and Tonia decide to leave. They plan to live at the estate of Tonia's grandfather, which is close to the town of Yuriatin.

Chapter Seven: Train to the Urals

The train ride is long, uncomfortable, and dangerous. Paranoia reigns everywhere in the government, in the military, and among the citizens. Yurii and his family must travel in a boxcar. The passenger cars are reserved for soldiers who are being taken to the frontlines.

Just before they arrive at Yuriatin, Yurii decides to take a walk at night when the train stops. Guards suspect him of being a spy or a deserter and take him to the man in charge. This man is known by the name Strelnikov. He is feared by everyone. He is a fierce fighter and renowned military strategist. He is also known as a cold-blooded killer. Yurii is interrogated by Strelnikov, who later muses about a wife and daughter who live in Yuriatin. Strelnikov wonders if they are still there. Yurii believes this man is Pasha, Lara's lost husband.

Chapter Eight: Arrival

Yurii is told that the old Krueger place where he and Tonia were heading is now occupied by a man named Mikulitsyn, who was once a manager at Krueger's ironworks. Yurii is warned that Mikulitsyn might turn Yurii and Tonia away. Both Yurii and Tonia are viewed suspiciously because they come from a moneyed class at a time when the labor class and peasants are in power. Yurii also finds out about the partisans, a group of fighters who infiltrate foreign forces (Hungarian and German, for instance) who are attacking the outer fringes of the Soviet Union. One band of the partisans in the area of Yuriatin is called the Forest Brotherhood because they camp in the thick woods in that area. The leader of the Brotherhood is Livka (or Liberius), the son of Mikulitsyn, the man living in the old Krueger estate.

Yurii and his family must go by horse from

Yuriatin to the smaller town of Varykino, where Tonia's grandfather's house and factory are located. When they first meet Mikulitsyn in Varykino, Yurii and Tonia are a bit dismayed. Mikulitsyn is afraid that Yurii and Tonia will only bring trouble upon his family. However, he offers to allow them to stay in what used to be an old manager's house behind the main estate. Yurii and Tonia prepare to spend their time there as farmers, producing their own food, and generally keeping to themselves.

Chapter Nine: Varykino

Yurii and his family have happily settled in Varykino. They are living quietly as farmers, dependent only on the land. One day, while Yurii is visiting the library in Yuriatin, he recognizes Lara, sitting across the room. He decides not to approach her. After she leaves, Yurii walks over to the pile of books that Lara had been reading and notices her address on a piece of papers. Time passes, and one day Yurii decides to find Lara's house on another visit into town. He runs into her and admits that he had seen her earlier. She confesses that she saw him, too. As they drink some tea together in Lara's house, Lara confirms that the man called Strelnikov whom Yurii had met while on the train was indeed Pasha, Lara's husband. She and Pasha have not been together, however, since the day that Pasha left to join the army. Lara has accepted that for some unknown reason, Pasha believes he must not give away his identity. Yurii decides to spend the night, making some excuse to Tonia for not coming home.

He feels like a criminal, but he cannot help loving Lara. On his way home one night, a few months later, Yurii is kidnapped by soldiers of the Forest Brotherhood.

Chapter Ten: The Highway

Yurii is taken to a place in Siberia where the Soviet government has been overthrown by banned Cossacks, former political prisoners, and other forgotten soldiers in the Soviet armies. At one time, this far northern area was under the control of a Siberian provisional government, but Yurii learns that it is now under the loose direction of an Admiral Kolchak. This chapter presents background regarding the politicians who are struggling to rule this part of Russia. There are partisans, whose members are loyal to the Red Army, who include Liberius, Tiverzin, and Pasha's father. There are members of the White Army, the more conservative wing of landowners and merchants. One faction fights another. As one citizen puts it, all the good young men have been lost. Those who are left are merely the garbage. Various divisions within these groups argue about what direction they should take.

Chapter Eleven: The Forest Brotherhood

Yurii has been gone from his family for over a year. He is with the partisans, acting as the group's physician. He is not treated as a prisoner, but he knows he cannot leave. He has tried to escape three times. He is constantly on the move with this group. Yurii spends several nights, sleeping in the same trench as Liberius, who keeps him up all night with his chatter. Liberius is addicted to cocaine, which Yurii has kept as a medical treatment for wounded soldiers. Yurii tries to keep his political comments to himself, but at one time, he tells Liberius, who is a zealous communist, that the theory of communism and the practice of it are far different things. Liberius then tells Yurii that rumors have it that Varykino has been attacked and destroyed by the White Army. Yurii fears for his family.

Time passes. Russia experiences the October Revolution on October 25, 1917, during which the Bolsheviks, led by Vladimir Lenin, take over the government.

Chapter Twelve: The Rowan Tree

The White Army has completely surrounded the partisans, who rally and break through the White Army's ranks. Refugees from the villages pour in before the White Army recuperates and cuts off the path, leaving part of the partisans stranded. News arrives that the newest revolution is over. The White Army is in retreat. The partisans join ranks with the Red Army, which is demolishing Kolchak's grip on Siberia. Yurii learns that most of the inhabitants of Varykino escaped before the White Army destroyed the village. Yurii hopes that his family has returned to Moscow and imagines the struggle that Tonia must have endured. Before he was kidnapped, Yurii had learned that Tonia was pregnant. He wonders about her having given birth. Yuriatin, where Lara is, however, appears to be still in tact. Yurii decides one night that he must escape from the partisans.

Chapter Thirteen: Opposite the House of Sculptures

Yurii finally arrives in Yuriatin, a "wild-looking, emaciated man." He has been walking for months. He finds Lara's house empty, but a note from her suggests that she is still in the area. He finally collapses there, falling in and out of dreams. When he finally regains consciousness, he finds he has been unconscious for many days. Lara has been taking care of him. After he regains his strength, he works at the local hospital. Yurii sends several letters to Tonia and finally receives a reply. She has given birth to a daughter, but the family will soon be deported.

Chapter Fourteen: Return to Varykino

Komarovsky arrives in town. He has come to warn both Lara and Yurii that their names are on a list of suspicious people. They will be imprisoned, maybe even shot, if they do not get away. Komarovsky is in a position of power with the government. He offers to take them away. Lara and Yurii refuse. Instead they decide to move back to the old Krueger place in Varykino, where Yurii and Tonia used to live. They stay there for a month or so, before Komarovsky comes again. Yurii suggests that Lara go with Komarovsky for her daughter's sake. Yurii promises to join them soon. After Lara leaves, Strelnikov (Pasha) shows up. Yurii tells him that Lara loves Pasha above all else. Pasha tells Yurii to run. Government forces are shooting anyone they fear is against them. In the night, Yurii hears a shot. In the morning he finds Pasha dead in the snow, an apparent suicide.

Chapter Fifteen: Conclusion

At the beginning of the New Economic Plan (NEP), Yurii returns to Moscow. The NEP is what the narrator calls "the most ambiguous and hypocritical of all Soviet periods," a time during which the ban on private enterprise is lifted in order to increase Soviet productivity. It is 1922, and Yurii returns to the city a broken man. At his side is a young man, a survivor of all the wars in Siberia, Vasia Brykin, who helps Yurii on their long walk toward Moscow. As time passes, Yurii and Vasia find means of making money. Yurii turns to writing. Vasia watches as Yurii turns more and more inward, away from life and passion.

After settling in, Yurii is further disappointed by his former friends, who are, in Yurii's eyes, mere shadows of the people they once were. Yurii lives with a common-law wife, Marina Markel, who bears him two children. At one point, unable to fit into society and wanting to refresh himself, Yurii goes into seclusion, leaving notes behind to explain his need for privacy. He works on his writing, and one day collapses on the streets, dead. At his funeral, Lara reappears for a few days and then vanishes. The narrator suggests that Lara is taken away to a concentration camp.

Chapter Sixteen: Epilogue

In the summer of 1943, Misha Gordon is involved in World War II. He is talking to a friend about a young girl who has suddenly appeared in his life. The girl's name is Tania, and she has a smile that Gordon finds similar to Yurii's. She tells her story to Gordon and to Evgraf Zhivago, Yurii's half-brother, who is now a general. Tania is an orphan of the war. She never knew her father and was long since separated from her mother, either because her mother was kidnapped or because her mother gave her away. She is not sure. Both men realize that Tania is the daughter of Yurii and Lara. Evgraf promises to take care of her.

Chapter Seventeen: The Poems of Yurii Zhivago

The last section is a collection of Yurii's poems, unaccompanied by narrative or explanation.

Characters

Pasha Antipov

Pasha Antipov develops a crush on Lara at a very early age. Eventually he marries her in Moscow then shortly afterward they leave for the village of Yuriatin in the Ural Mountains. After fathering a daughter, Pasha becomes restless and believes that joining the army will revive his passion for life. Rumors spread of his death or possible imprisonment. Pasha later turns up as the mysterious Strelnikov, leader of a group of extremists of the new Russian government.

Pasha has decided to completely disconnect from his former life and never sees Lara or his daughter again, although he is often stationed close to Yuriatin, where they live. At the end of the story, Pasha and Yurii meet. Pasha knows that Yurii has had an affair with Lara. But Yurii tells Pasha that Lara admitted to him that it was Pasha to whom she owed her allegiance. Shortly after this, Pasha kills himself.

Vasia Brykin

Vasia Brykin is a young man, the victim of war. He comes across Yurii as the doctor is walking back to Moscow at the end of the story. Vasia becomes disappointed in Yurii as he watches the doctor withdraw from life. Vasia represents the generation of young people who have learned to make a life for themselves in the midst of war, poverty, and stringent government regulations.

Lieutenant Galiullin

Lieutenant Galiullin appears when Lara and Yurii are working in the hospital on the frontlines. He tells Lara that Pasha was not killed but rather was taken prisoner. Galiullin works with Lara and Yurii for awhile then disappears. Later he reappears as a leader of the White Army. Whereas he had at one time considered himself a good friend of Pasha, he ends up the leader of an army that is opposed to Pasha's group.

Misha Gordon

Misha Gordon grew up with Yurii at the Gromekos' house. He is in and out of Yurii's life throughout the novel, one of the few acquaintances of Yurii's still alive at the end. Yurii was once very close to Misha, but as they mature, Yurii finds Misha artificial, willing to go along with the dictates of the government and too afraid to challenge them.

Alexander Gromeko

Alexander Gromeko is Tonia's father. Yurii greatly admires this man, a chemistry professor, who raised him. Alexander comes to live with Yurii and Tonia after they are married. Yurii often turns to Alexander, appreciating the way his fatherin-law thinks.

Anna Gromeko

Anna was Tonia's mother and Alexander's wife. She is very loving toward Yurii and suggests that Tonia and Yurii become engaged. Anna dies early in the novel.

Antonina Gromeko

Antonina Gromeko, called Tonia, is Alexander's and Anna's daughter. She is also the granddaughter of Ivan Krueger, the rich industrialist from Varykino, to whose house Tonia and Yurii escape when Moscow's economy collapses. Tonia bears Yurii a son and persuades Yurii to escape from Moscow, fearful that because they both come from moneyed families, they will be persecuted by the new communist regime. Tonia bears up well, knowing that Yurii has fallen in love with Lara, sending notes to Lara when she needs to find out where Yurii is. Tonia spends two uninterrupted periods with Yurii, but for the rest of the novel, Yurii is often absent from her. Tonia becomes pregnant with a second child and gives birth after Yurii is kidnapped by the partisans. She escapes to Moscow but is later deported with the rest of her family, presumably ending up in Paris. She is never heard from after that.

Amalia Guishar

Amalia Guishar, the widow of a rich, French businessman, is the mother of Lara and Rodia. Amalia arrives in Moscow to begin a new life with the help of her husband's old lawyer, Victor Komarovsky. She opens a sewing shop, but when the women in her shop go on strike and when Amalia finds out that Lara is having an affair with Komarovsky, Amalia tries to commit suicide.

Larisa Guishar

Larisa Guishar, called Lara, is sixteen years old when she first appears in this story. She begins an affair with Komarovsky and is both attracted and appalled by it. Later, after she has broken away from his control over her, she tries to kill him.

After graduating from college, Lara asks Pasha to marry her. She then suggests that they get away from Moscow and go to the village of Yuriatin in the Urals. She gives birth to Pasha's child. When Pasha enlists in the army and goes missing, Lara goes to the frontlines to look for him. She meets Yurii there and is drawn to him. The passion she feels for Yurii is almost out of her control, despite the fact that she truly still loves Pasha.

Strong, independent, and intelligent, Lara thrives on her own. However, when Yurii turns up several years later, she cannot resist him. She helps to nurse him back to health and continues her affair with him, even though Yurii's family lives close by.

When Yurii goes missing for almost two years, Lara waits for him. She is there when he returns, a sick man, and nurses him back to health again. She lives with Yurii, but she knows that she and he are marked people and could likely be imprisoned or put to death. When Komarovsky comes to Lara and offers her a way out of her predicament, Lara refuses to go with him. Only when she believes that Yurii will follow does Lara leave to preserve her safety and that of her daughter.

Lara reappears at the story's end. By this time Pasha is dead and so is Yurii. Then Lara disappears, supposedly accused of being an enemy of the Soviet government and taken to a concentration camp for women. Readers learn in the epilogue that she gave birth to Yurii's daughter, Tania.

Rodia Guishar

Rodia Guishar is Lara's younger brother. His role in this story is minimal. He gets into trouble and needs money, which forces Lara to turn to Komarovsky.

Uncle Kolia

See Nikolai Vedeniapin

Victor Komarovsky

Victor Komarovsky is portrayed as a cold-blooded businessman who takes advantage of women, especially young ones. It is suggested that he might have caused Yurii's father to lose his fortune and commit suicide. Victor does whatever he needs to do to survive, without consideration of morals or a twinge of conscience. He has an affair with both Lara's mother and Lara. Later he appears in the story when Lara and Yurii have been placed on a list of suspicious persons who will be arrested and imprisoned if not executed. Victor pleads with Lara to go to the farther boundaries of Siberia where he will protect her. Lara does go with him after she is tricked into believing that Yurii will follow. Victor lives with Lara for several years.

Ivan Krueger

Ivan Krueger is Anna Gromeko's rich father and Tonia's grandfather. Ivan made his money in iron and owned a large factory and huge family estate, to which Tonia and Yurii escape when Moscow collapses during the Bolshevik Revolution.

Livka

See Liberius Mikulitsyn

Marina Markel

Marina Markel is the daughter of a man who used to work for Yurii. Upon returning to Moscow at the end of the story, Yurii shares a house with Markel, who treats Yurii as being beneath him. Marina takes pity of Yurii and eventually falls in love with him. They live together as man and wife and Marina bears him two children.

Mikulitsyn

At one time Mikulitsyn was a manager in Ivan Krueger's iron factory in Varykino. When Yurii and Tonia run away from Moscow, they find Mikulitsyn living in the old Krueger estate. Mikulitsyn is a small time political official in the town and agrees to shelter Yurii and his family.

Liberius Mikulitsyn

Liberius is Mikulitsyn's son, who becomes the leader of the Partisans who kidnap Yurii.

Strelnikov

See Pasha Antipov

Tania

Tania shows up in the Epilogue, when the Soviet Union is fighting in World War II. Misha Gordon comes across her and is drawn to her because of her smile, which Misha compares to the type of smile Yurii had. Tania is interrogated by Evgraf Zhivago, Yurii's half brother, who is now a general in the Soviet military. Upon listening to Tania's story, he realizes that she is the daughter of Yurii and Lara. Evgraf promises to take care of the young girl. Tania remembers her mother but never knew her father.

Kuprian Tiverzin

Kuprian Tiverzin appears in the beginning of the story, one of the instigators of the strikes that sweep across Russia right before the collapse of the Russian tsar. He becomes a leader in the Red Army.

Nikolai Vedeniapin

Nikolai Vedeniapin is Yurii's maternal uncle. In the beginning of the story, Nikolai is Yurii's hero. Nikolai is responsible for the boy after Yurii's father and mother die. However, by the time Yurii is a teen, Nikolai has given Yurii to the Gromekos.

After Nikolai has become a famous author, Yurii is proud of him and the way he thinks. Nikolai has taught Yurii to open his mind to new possibilities, a concept that Yurii develops. However, Nikolai is ultimately a victim of the newly established communistic government that discourages individual thought. In the end, Yurii is disappointed with his uncle.

Andrei Zhivago

Andrei Zhivago, Yurii Zhivago's father, was, at one time, a very rich and influential industrialist. He deserted his family and lived with another woman. Yurii very rarely saw his father. In the first chapter of the story, Andrei commits suicide by throwing himself off a train.

Evgraf Zhivago

Evgraf Zhivago, Yurii's half-brother, is the product of Yurii's father's affair. Evgraf appears at times when Yurii is in trouble, such as when he falls sick with typhus. He also appears at the end of the story as an influential general in the Soviet army. He promises to take care of Tania, the daughter of Yurii and Lara.

Maria Zhivago

Maria Zhivago is Yurii Zhivago's mother. The novel begins with Maria's funeral.

Yura Zhivago

See Yurii Zhivago

Yurii Zhivago

Yurii Zhivago is the protagonist. The novel encompasses Yurii's development from young boyhood to professional doctor. Yurii has high ideals and expects much from what he perceives as the changing political mode of communism, which he expects to take over the world. As the story progresses, however, Yurii sees the ravages of war and the brutal behavior of the leaders. His initial ideals and optimism do not match the reality of how practitioners of communism plan out the lives of the

Russian citizens. As the story progresses, Yurii withdraws more and more into himself.

Just as Yurii is torn between the ideals of political theory and the reality of its practice, he is torn between the love for Tonia, his wife, who represents the conventional relationship in marriage, and his love of Lara, which inspires a illicit passion that Yurii likens to natural urgings. Unable to choose between the two women, Yurii eventually withdraws from both of them.

By the end of the story, Yurii has withdrawn from society, from the two women who matter most to him, and from his children and his friends. He has withdrawn from society and into his writing. In the end, he lives in a small room where he sorts through and records his thoughts. He dies on a public sidewalk away from everyone he has ever known.

Themes

Revolution

Revolution effects the violent and sudden change of political order, and Pasternak's novel shows its all-encompassing effects. Various uprisings and civil and world wars create the backdrop for and determine much of the action. The characters' lives are shaped by political upheaval. Revolution heightens the ironic contrast between the initial ideal and the harsh outcome. Revolution causes destruction and suffering and illustrates the contest between powerful groups and individuals. Revolution shows how the ordinary individual is swept along by group action. The characters fall for the hypnotic promise in political rhetoric, and they suffer the ruthless havoc that follows. Pasternak's portrait of revolution and the destruction it caused prevented his novel from being published in his country. He was called a traitor because he presented a critical view of this troubled time in Russian history. This more negative view was not permitted.

But Pasternak also depicts some positives in his portrait of revolution. He shows how passionately people believed in bringing about change and how willing they were to make sacrifices. Although he describes massacres, he also depicts the undying hope that some of the people involved in the revolution could maintain in spite of constant fighting.

Topics for Further Study

- Watch any of the televised versions or the 1965 movie adaptation of *Doctor Zhivago* with your class. Then lead a class discussion on how the adaptation varies from the written text. Use some of the following questions to get the discussion going. Then add some of your own questions. What themes are emphasized in the adaptation? Does the movie elicit different responses than the book? Is the characterization of Yurii different in the movie than it is in the novel? What role does the affair between Yurii and Lara play in the movie?

How does that differ from the novel? At the end of the discussion, take a poll. Ask your peers which presentation they like best, the novel or the movie, and have them discuss the reasons behind their preference.

- Do a historical presentation in which you compare the timeline in Pasternak's novel, which sometimes runs counter to actual historical events, with the history of the Bolshevik Revolution. Compare a map of old Russia with one of the Soviet Union, and explain the changes in the country. Locate the major battles and explain who fought in them, so your classmates better understand such groups as the Cossacks, the Partisans, and the White and the Red Armies.

- Research communism as a political theory. How is the communist economy supposed to work? Why was there widespread starvation and lack of supplies as Lenin, and then Stalin, tried to set up a communist state in the Soviet Union? Present your findings to your class.

- Take what little description that Pasternak gives his readers of the main characters, Yurii, Lara, and Tonia, and draw sketches or portraits of them as you imagined them. Present your drawings to your class. Ask them how your images compare to what they imagined.

Ideal versus Real

When the ideal clashes with the real, which it often does, alternative plans or concepts must be made. One of Pasternak's criticisms of the communist revolution in Russia was that these alternative plans were suppressed. The ideal, as Pasternak demonstrates in this novel, remains a concept or idea; it cannot be realized in actual circumstances. Pasternak presents the ideal in politics, economics, love, and friendship. When his characters attempt to bring the ideal into their lives, they show that it is impossible. Political upheaval brings death as citizens attempt to reshape their government in accord with the highest ideals of socialism and communism. When confronted or obstructed, reform leaders were brutal and resorted to dictatorship. When economic ideals were put in place, businesses dried up, people went hungry, and corruption spread. Even those intellectuals who first discovered and promoted the ideals got lost in their own ideas and stagnated. Zhivago himself discovers that his love relationships are not ideal; with one person he knows the dryness of an intellectual love and with the other the emotional and moral chaos of an illicit affair. People have flaws, Pasternak seems to imply, and ideals may spur them to act, but ideals themselves are not realized in actual experience.

Destruction and Suffering

Destruction and the suffering it causes can bring out the best or the worst in characters, either forcing them to rise as heroes or reducing them to beggars. The war touches everyone; suffering is universal. Characters suffer the loss of loved ones, homes, and basic needs for survival such as food and shelter. Wars provide the most obvious mode of destruction but not all destruction happens on the battlefield. The death of his parents destroys Zhivago's inner peace and security. The loss of wealth leads Zhivago's father to commit suicide. Health is destroyed when rats infest dwellings and easily contaminate the paltry food supply, which spreads disease. There is also the destruction of hope as brutal leaders, drunk on power, make extreme demands on the common people. Throughout all the destruction and suffering, however, Pasternak demonstrates how people adjust. Death of a loved one occurs, but those who are left behind learn to live without that person. Wealth of the bourgeois is stripped, and people learn to live on much less.

Individual versus Group

Socialism and communism promote the group over the individual. Although some ideas in socialism and communism seem to recommend helping the poor, the country peasants, and the working class, Pasternak, through his protagonist, shows that thinking as a group rather than as individuals leads not only to stagnation but also to poorly conceived ideas. As communism spreads throughout his country, Zhivago feels more and more isolated from his former intellectual friends. They wear masks or enact prescribed roles rather than moving forward, independently. They begin thinking as a group rather than as individuals. As individuals, Zhivago believes, they might have thought up productive solutions. They might have found answers for starvation or ways to avoid or cope with the typhus epidemic. Perhaps these catastrophes could have been avoided if people had not been afraid to think for themselves, Zhivago concludes.

Style

The Classic Russian Novel

Pasternak's *Doctor Zhivago* was written at the end of what many critics refer to as the golden age of Russian literature. Although the novel differs in some ways from the works of Tolstoy and Dostoyevsky, there are enough similarities to see it as following the form of the traditional nineteenth-century Russian novel.

The classic Russian novel provides extensive historical details. It also tends to explore religion and depict its influence on the characters. The large nineteenth-century Russian novel is realistic; it determines to present the authentic truth of real life. Often there are discussions of philosophy and contrasts drawn between the lives of those who dwell in the city and those who make their homes in the country. These novels also distinguish between romantic ideals and brute realism. The story of families is told, their ancestry and their progeny.

Journal Writing

Often in this novel, the narrator or some of the main characters reveal their thoughts as if they were writing in a journal. Quotation marks are even used to imply that the entries were taken directly from the journal. This adds a personal or introspective look into the characters' minds and also adds legitimacy to their comments or observations. It makes readers feel privy to the inner thoughts of the characters. It also helps the reader to imagine that the characters are real. The journal writings add complexity to the characters, as they are not just reacting outwardly to what is happening to them in the story but are also taking the time to think privately through the larger issues that define their experiences.

Compare & Contrast

- **1910s:** Russia suffers through a series of civil revolutions as the people attempt to gain democratic rights and overthrow the rule of the tsar. The country suffers from devastating losses in World War I.

  1950s: Russia (now called the U.S.S.R.) is involved in a cold war with the United States.

  Today: Russia has witnessed the dissolution of the Soviet Union and struggles between communist rule and capitalism. The Russian Orthodox Church declares Nicholas II, the last Russian tsar, a saint.

- **1910s:** Lenin takes Marxist ideas and creates a political philosophy upon which the Soviet Union's

Communist Party is based.

1950s: Mao Zedong is established as the leader of a new communist government in China. In the United States, meanwhile, the U.S. House of Representatives, under the influence of Joseph McCarthy who heads its Committee on Un-American Activities, attempts to purge any communist sympathizers from the country.

Today: Kim Jong Il, leader of North Korea, struggles to maintain control in his communist country, whose military is one of the world's largest but whose people suffer from starvation.

- **1910s:** There is a political revolution in Russia as the people rebel against the monarchy.

  1950s: Europe and the United States witness the beginnings of a cultural revolution as the younger generation rebels against the ideals of the older generation.

  Today: Many countries witness acts of terrorism, some of which are based on or prompted by particular religious beliefs.

Some critics have argued that the entire text of *Doctor Zhivago* is one large journal, the exposition of the author's thoughts, thinly clothed in characterization and plot. In other words, the novel does not fit into the expected form. The characters are not fully developed and the plotline barely exists. The main purpose in the novel is to express the ruminations of the author. The dialogue is not so much a form of communication between two characters as it is a monologue that the author records, perhaps for readers, maybe just for himself, as one might write to oneself in a diary.

Epic

Many people have called Pasternak's novel an epic. Traditionally, an epic refers to a long poem, but in modern times, this term has been used to describe novels and even movies. In general, an epic is a large work that encompasses a complex, huge subject. While it may focus on particular individuals, an epic generally tells the story of a people or a race, often including the story of how a given civilization or society had its beginning.

In an epic, the hero represents or endures the challenges that the people of his country face. While Zhivago, toward the end of this novel, feels more like an outsider than a hero leading his people, readers may envision him as a man of or before his time. Zhivago suffers much like most of the people in his country and is not afraid to speak his mind. He sees the foibles of the newly empowered leaders as well as the weaknesses and fears that paralyze many of the intelligentsia. In many ways, Zhivago predicts the fall of the Soviet Union, and in that sense, he may be considered heroic.

An epic may also cover a large geographic area and time. The timeframe of this novel, especially when read in the twenty-first century, adds to its epic quality. Also, the protagonist travels the vast landscape of the Soviet Union from its famous cities of Moscow and St. Petersburg to the remote regions of the Ural Mountains and Siberia.

However, *Doctor Zhivago* fails to meet the definition of an epic in the fact that it does not focus on great, majestic heroes or fantastic kings and warriors, but rather on the ordinary citizen, the true subject of an idealized communist state.

Historical Context

Karl Marx (1818-1883)

Pasternak studied philosophy in school while he was in Germany and was interested, as many students were at that time, in the writings of Karl Marx, a German philosopher who supported the working class and whose ideas fueled the socialist movement that began in the early twentieth century and swept across the world.

In *Economic and Philosophical Manuscripts* (1844) Marx contrasted the different approaches to labor under a capitalist government and a communist one. In Marx's ideal communist environment, laborers worked in a cooperative in which all shared equally in the benefits. Together with Friedrich Engels (1820-1895), Marx published a book from which many revolutionists took their ideas. The *Communist Manifesto* (1847) contained all of Marx's beliefs about the nature of a communist society. This book was written in a simple language, unlike some of Marx's other works. The publication quickly became very popular and was said to be one of the instigations of revolutions that began sweeping across Europe. Marx's most extensive work, on which he devoted the latter years of his life, was the three-volume *Das Kapital* in which Marx delineated a capitalist society and its effects upon workers. Volumes one and two were published in 1885. After Marx's death, Engels put together Marx's notes and published the third volume in 1895.

Maxim Gorky (1868-1936)

Pasternak was also influenced by the political works of Maxim Gorky. Gorky was the pseudonym, taken from the Russian word that means "bitter," used by Aleksei Maksimovich Peshkov. Gorky began as a journalist and spent many years traveling across the vast territory of Russia, and what the standards of living he saw agitated him. To make sense of his experiences and to sort through his responses to them, he began writing fiction, which became instantly popular. His first work, *Sketches and Stories* (1889) tells of the hardships of the working class, of social outcasts, and the poor. Gorky's best known work is a play that he conceived after being encouraged by famed Russian playwright Anton Chekhov. Gorky's play, *The Lower Depths* (1902), received a lot of attention in Russia and also found appreciative audiences in Europe and in the United States.

In the same year that his play was positively received, Gorky was banished to northern Russia because of his political activism and his revolutionary ideas. He joined the leftist group, the Social Democratic Party led by Lenin. Then in 1906, Gorky traveled to the United States to raise money for the Bolsheviks. Later, he would find both the Bolsheviks' and Lenin's theories too harsh, and he placed himself in voluntary exile from his homeland. Gorky returned to Russia, however, before his death. By then Stalin's regime was in full force. Under Stalin, intellectuals and artists, along with many other citizens, were considered suspicious and thousands were executed. When Gorky died suddenly in 1936, rumors spread that he had been poisoned.

Vladimir Lenin (1870-1924)

The first head of the Soviet Union, Vladimir Lenin (whose real name was Vladimir Ilyich Ulyanov) was the son of a Russian official who worked to improve the education of the masses. Lenin's brother was hanged as a terrorist, and his sister, who was considered an accomplice, was exiled. These events are said to have radicalized the intelligent Lenin, turning his thoughts to revolution. A student of Marxism, Lenin was himself exiled in 1895 for five years for contributing to propaganda in favor of revolution. His most famous propaganda pamphlet, "What Is to Be Done," is said to have sparked the 1903 split between the two factions of the Russian Social-Democratic Labour Party. The Mensheviks disagreed with Lenin's philosophy, while the Bolsheviks completely embraced it and made Lenin their leader. Another important and influential writing was Lenin's *Materialism and Empiriocriticism* (1909), which espoused the basic tenets of the Marxist-Leninist political philosophy. Lenin led the October Revolution in 1917, which overran the provisional government and then took power. He was elected chairman of the Council of People's Commissioners. After two assassination attempts on his life, in 1918, Lenin took a heavy handed and deadly approach to suppressing any rebellion against him and his government. Censorship prevented counterrevolutionary publications, and many people suspected of being against Lenin's revolution were executed, deported, or imprisoned. Known as the Red Terror, this systematic abuse of human rights continued for years. Some scholars estimate that approximately 6,300 were killed the first year; by 1921, an estimated 70,000 had been imprisoned in what came to be called the Gulag, a network of labor camps and prisons across remote areas of the country.

Lenin died of a stroke in 1924, and his body went on permanent display in the Lenin Mausoleum in Red Square in Moscow. Later, he was revered as the first leader of a communist state and was honored by statues in almost every Russian city. The name of St. Petersburg was changed to Leningrad until the fall of the Soviet Union in 1991.

Alexander Pushkin (1799-1837)

Considered Russia's greatest poet (and often referred to in Pasternak's book), Pushkin is also credited with establishing Russian literature. Pushkin was the first to use the language of the people in his poetry, thus making it accessible to the general public. He was the child of aristocrats, born in Moscow, and was a published poet by the age of fourteen. His earliest writings were influenced by old Russian fairytales. Pushkin was a radical politically and was later banished from his town because of his philosophy expressed in some of his writing. In 1833, Pushkin published what is considered his most influential work, a novel told in verse, titled *Evgenii Onegin*. His writings, with their mix of satire and drama continued to influence Russian literature for generations.

First Russian Revolution, 1905

Dissatisfaction among Russian workers was festering before 1905. Revolutionaries and those who called for democratic reform were carefully watched and if necessary suppressed, which caused a large emigration of intellectuals, artists, and students from Russia to other European countries. Many of these self-exiled people learned about Karl Marx while living in Germany, France, and Italy, and incorporated his ideas into their own beliefs about political change. In 1898, the Marxist Russian Social-Democratic Labour Party was formed. This party split into two factions in 1902, the Bolsheviks and the Mensheviks. In the following few years, many top Russian officials were assassinated, causing the government to crack down even harder on anyone suspected of being a revolutionary. During this same time, Russia was involved in a losing war with Japan. The people became more and more dissatisfied with the poor conditions of their lives, and even peasants began burning down farms. As a result, a large part of the Russian Army was involved in suppressing fellow citizens.

On January 22, 1905, a quiet protest march in St. Petersburg to complain about the poor living conditions and to ask for voting rights began moving down the streets toward the winter residence of Tsar Nicholas II. The crowd was confronted by armed men on horseback who shot out indiscriminately. In the end, around one thousand people were killed with many more thousands injured. This confrontation and massacre, which became known as Bloody Sunday, sparked even more widespread protests across the country. Workers organized strikes, peasants looted the homes of gentry, and even landowners demanded access to more land. The government made slight concessions, reducing forced labor and insubstantial payments for work and setting up a powerless representative arm of the government, which only infuriated the people further. In October of 1905, the people presented their October Manifesto, which demanded more civil rights.

Nicholas II reluctantly signed the manifesto, giving the people the right to form political parties and take part in the government. Their role was minor, and the Duma (the political house of representatives) was completely suppressed by the tsar a year later. The police and the military quickly took up arms against anyone suspected of political activism, yet the political activists increased their attacks on government officials. However, nothing really changed. The tsar continued his absolute rule, the peasants and laborers continued to suffer and go hungry, and the unrest simmered without a leader or powerful organization to focus its energy.

Russian Revolution of 1917

By 1917, the Russian people were dismayed. Thousands of people had died in Russia's disastrous involvement in World War I. Soldiers were deserting from the army by the thousands. Many returned home and used their weapons to take land they did not own. Food was scarce, and riots broke out in St. Petersburg. Soldiers united with the rioters, and this time they were successful in removing Nicholas II from power. Nicholas was forced to abdicate; he was assassinated the following year, along with all members of his immediate family and some members of the staff. He was the last Russian tsar.

With the tsar gone, a provisional government was established, which leaned toward a democratic form. However, the provisional government only lasted until October when the Bolsheviks, led by Vladimir Lenin, took power and established the Soviet Union in a nearly bloodless coup. This became known as the October Revolution. The Bolsheviks were popular but did not represent the majority of Russian citizens; the Bolsheviks knew that they could not maintain rule by democratic vote, so they declared a dictatorship.

Russian Civil War, 1918-1920

The Bolsheviks were in power in 1918, having created the Union of Soviet Socialist Republics (U.S.S.R.). The Bolsheviks were members of the Russian Social Democratic Workers Party, which supported the political philosophy of Marx and the leadership of Lenin. The army that supported the Bolsheviks was called the Red Army. There was, however, an anti-Bolsheviks group that was referred to as the White Army, which represented the conservative wing of Russian political activists. The Russian Civil War was fought between these two groups. The Red Army had control of the cities of St. Petersburg and Moscow, while the White Army found support in the outlying areas. In order to counter the anti-Bolshevik movement, the Bolsheviks created a secret police organization that captured, imprisoned, and killed anyone suspected of allegiance with the White Army. This became known as the Campaign of Red Terror. The fight between the two armies lasted for two years, then ended when the Red Army was successful in completely putting down the White Army in 1920.

Critical Overview

Boris Pasternak was awarded the Nobel Prize for literature in 1958, but he was forbidden by the Russian government from accepting it, and *Doctor Zhivago* was initially banned from Russia. Pasternak's novel, however, won widespread acceptance and appreciation all over the world.

In his introduction to the 1991 edition of *Doctor Zhivago*, John Bayley attributes the great force of the novel to the "poetic power of the hero," Yurii Zhivago, and to Pasternak's skill in being "able to fill the book with that richness and minutiae of life which distinguish[es] a great novel." In the 1980s and 1990s, Bayley writes, readers and critics enjoy Pasternak's fiction more for its art than for its politics, while during the 1950s cold war between the Soviet Union and the United States the politics mattered most. "Thirty years or so after the book's first publication in English," Bayley writes, "it is the feeling of poetry it gives which now makes its strongest impression, an impression of continuing vitality and greatness…. No longer the explosive cry of freedom and protest from the heart of Stalin's Russia, the book has been published in its own country and been soberly valued and appraised, taking a distinctive and distinguished place in the tradition of Russian literary art." Bayley then explains the novel's uniqueness: *Doctor Zhivago* "is one of those rare works—whether we consider it fiction, poetry, or a kind of imaginary autobiography—which makes no attempt to protect itself against the reactions of the reader. It does not seem to care whether we are moved or unmoved by it; whether we criticize its sentiment and its discourse or whether we surrender to them. Like life itself it goes on its own way, indifferent to the conflicting responses of those who are, as it were, living it. This is an extremely rare quality in a modern novel, for modern fiction is the most self-conscious of art forms."

In *Pasternak: A Critical Study*, Henry Gifford comments on the fact that Pasternak was a poet who wrote a novel. Gifford states, "Though Pasternak would have liked it to be otherwise, he was 'first and last a poet, a lyric poet.' Dramatically, his novel lacks power; it is not everywhere realized with the same adequacy." Yet Gifford praises Pasternak for his "extraordinary keenness and fertility of perception," concluding that "*Doctor Zhivago* is a poet's novel." Finally, Gifford writes: "That intensity is focused finally in the poems proper that form the last section of the book, and for which the novel has provided an elaborate context."

What Do I Read Next?

- Pasternak thought of himself primarily as a poet. A selection of his poetry appeared in *Pasternak: Selected Poems*, published in 1992.

- *War and Peace*, first published in a series between 1863 and 1869, covers the lives of several characters and the Russian culture during the Napoleonic wars. Tolstoy, a friend of Pasternak's father, is a Russian literary legend. This novel is an epic recollection of five families and how they were affected by the wars.

- *Crime and Punishment* is another classic Russian novel, written by Fyodor Dostoevsky and first published in 1866. The story takes place in St. Petersburg, Russia, and centers on a rebellious young student who commits a murder. This novel is much more than a murder mystery, however, as Dostoevsky uses the crime and the criminal to portray the ills of society.

- Alexander Solzhenitsyn's novel *One Day in the Life of Ivan Denisovich* (1962) relates the story of a man caught in the oppressive Stalin years in Russia. Like Pasternak, Solzhenitsyn was awarded a Nobel Prize for literature but was forbidden by his government from accepting it.

- A more contemporary award-winning Russian writer is Ludmila Ulitskaya, whose 2005 novella and collection of short stories *Sonechka* relates stories of love, often turned bad. Ulitskaya tells stories of families who try to make their lives work in a terribly dysfunctional society.

Angela Livingstone, in her critical study of *Doctor Zhivago*, reviews the praise and the troubles that Pasternak experienced when his book was first published. "In 1958," she writes, "people started talking about Pasternak all over the world. Journalists, literary critics, people in public life, writers and readers, all suddenly became interested in this Russian who had written a novel which his own country refused to publish." In Pasternak's own country, *Doctor Zhivago* "was denounced as an anti-Soviet work by large numbers of Soviet citizens who had not read it. Its author was attacked as a traitor and condemned in the Press and at writers' meetings in the most vituperative language." Livingstone adds: "While persecuted by his fellow-countrymen, Pasternak found himself winning friends in the rest of the world, receiving up to seventy foreign letters a day, most of which expressed admiration." Livingstone points out that critics have had trouble categorizing Pasternak's work, not knowing for sure what to call it. She lists various descriptions: "It has been called 'a rhapsody,' 'a kind of morality play,' 'an introspective epic,' 'a poet's novel,' 'an apocalyptic poem in the form of a novel,' yet also 'a political novel par excellence,' 'a love story for all time,' as well as 'one of the most original works of modern times.'"

Sources

Bayley, John, "Introduction," in *Doctor Zhivago*, Pantheon Books, 1991, pp. xii, xiii.

Gifford, Henry, "*Doctor Zhivago*," in *Pasternak: A Critical Study*, Cambridge University Press, 1977, p. 197.

Livingstone, Angela, "Reception, Importance, and Position of *Doctor Zhivago*," in *Doctor Zhivago*, Cambridge University Press, 1989, pp. 1, 2. 5.

Pasternak, Boris, *Doctor Zhivago*, Pantheon Books, 1958.

Further Reading

Barnes, Christopher, *Boris Pasternak: A Literary Biography*, Cambridge University Press, 2005.

> Using both personal accounts and family archives, Barnes depicts in this two-volume work both the personal and the political side of this great Russian writer.

Fitzpatrick, Sheila, *The Russian Revolution*, Oxford University Press, 2001.

> The Russian Revolution was supposed to bring about a model Marxist political form of government. Instead, the revolution caused great suffering among its intended beneficiaries. The research done by Fitzpatrick occurred after the fall of the Soviet Union, which opened up archives that had been closed to all historians, including Russian researchers, until this time.

Fleishman, Lazar, *Boris Pasternak: The Poet and His Politics*, Harvard University Press, 1990.

> Having researched Pasternak's politics in preparation for writing this book, Fleishman gives the reader an understanding of the times in which Pasternak lived and an

> appreciation of the courage Pasternak displayed in speaking his mind and standing up to government censorship.

Reid, Christopher, *From Tsar to Soviets: The Russian People and Their Revolution, 1917-21*, Oxford University Press, 1996.

> Reid presents the Russian Revolution through the eyes of the people, their struggles and their dreams. With a very readable style, Reid presents the political, economical, and social environment during the time of the Russian tsars and how the pressure built up in the citizenry, leading them to revolt. This book also attempts to explain how the Bolshevik goals differed from those of the citizens during the ensuing revolution.

Rudova, Larissa, *Understanding Boris Pasternak*, University of South Carolina Press, 1997.

> In this book, Rudova expands on the merits of Pasternak, claiming that Pasternak's literary ability and claim to fame extend well beyond this one publication. After all, in Russia, Pasternak is known first as a poet. Rudova explores Pasternak's proficiency and artistry foremost in this genre.

Lightning Source UK Ltd.
Milton Keynes UK
UKHW022309030521
383060UK00012B/2510

9 781375 398145